Feel Good
No Matter What

52 Inspiring Reflections to Awaken the Life You Love!

Dee
Your dedication
to passion is an
inspiration to me!
Wisdom & Energy!
Best Wishes
Anna

Nina Durfee

Anna Goldsworthy

WWR Press

Feel Good No Matter What: 52 Inspiring Reflections to Awaken the Life You Love!

Cover and Interior Design - Anna Goldsworthy

Printed in the United States by WWR Press
ISBN 978-0-6158991-8-3

First Printing, 2013

Also by Nina Durfee:

*Full Bloom: 7 Practical Steps to Get What You Want
+1 to Grow On*

Praise for
Feel Good No Matter What

Many of us spend our days dreaming about what our lives could be like "if only...." Another year passes by and our dreams remain out of reach. Feel Good No Matter What *helps us claim the life we've always wanted from our fullness, rather than from our fears.*

Fran Fisher, Master Certified Coach

My weekly dips into your Wisdom Well are the highlights of my week. The tips are presented with such a caring, personal tone and are so relevant, that I feel as though you have somehow read my mind. Thank you for sharing your wise insights.

Mary King-Petrik, Esthetic Services By Mary

With simple yet profound observations about the ways in which we often choose (yes, choose!) to get in our own way, Anna and Nina have created a compassionate guide to creating space and grace in our lives. As they share their own hard-won insights, it's easy to be inspired to look deeper at our own truth. I took away one bottom-line, powerful reminder: we teach others how to treat us. This book speaks from the heart and acts as a gentle coach, offering tips that will transform your awareness and lighten your load.

Beth Buelow, ACC, The Introvert Entrepreneur

The tip this week was so appropriate! We're cleaning out Mom's house, and everything seems to have emotional ties for me! I feel a renewed energy as I head out to tackle it again this morning. Thank you for a very timely reminder!

Janet

Feel Good No Matter What *is a thoughtful, inspirational journey into your Soul. Powerful questions invite you into an awareness of where you might be holding back on the "Good" in your life and offer an opportunity to breathe, retreat, and see things differently– no matter what! Beautifully written by two delightful women who have guided many on the journey of self-discovery and creating good in their lives.*

Kim Boyden, M.A., ChT, aVibrantPresence.com

Dedication

This work is dedicated to the power of partnering.

Acknowledgments

With deep appreciation we thank:

Diane and Melanie, our Tulip Sisters. You know why!

Joni Atkinson, professional photographer, personal friend, loyal retreat participant, and Dipper into the Wisdom Well.

Nancy Juetten, whose publicity expertise and enthusiasm inspired us to plant the seed for our first Dip into the Wisdom Well.

Linda L. Lane, whose gracious collaboration inspired us to creative endeavors we otherwise might not have attempted.

The brilliant instructors at the Academy for Coach Training (now InviteChange) in Bellevue, Washington, for holding us whole, capable and resourceful to discover our truths, craft our visions, declare our purposes, and graduate as Certified Professional Coaches.

All the amazing women who contributed patiently and openly to the adventure of birthing our cover: Georgia Anderson at Geneva's Interiors and Yvonne Atwell for facilitating an experience that lead to our ultimate choice; Dana Smith for holding our feet to the fire; and Melanie Kharrazi for intuitively capturing the perfect view two years in advance.

George Kao for his inspiration and his gracious introduction to Pamela Hale.

Pamela Hale for her encouragement to give way to the winds.

The countless courageous women who have blessed and continue to bless our lives and our livelihoods by allowing us to accompany them on their journeys of personal discovery and growth.

LaVerna J. Conrad (Anna's Mother and Nina's friend) for her inspiring example of lifelong dedication to her passion.

From Anna to Carmen for loving the crazy ones as much as I do, for adding girl power to our family, and for being beautifully and unapologetically you.

From Nina to Kristen and Kristin, for the dimension of love you have opened for my sons, and for the delightful female energy you add to our midst.

Our husbands and sons, whose love, trust, support, and good humor have added boundless joy to our lives, our processes, and our partnership!

Table of Contents

Preface

No matter how much pressure you feel at work, if you could find ways to relax for at least five minutes every hour, you'd be more productive.

Dr. Joyce Brothers

While attending a national conference many years ago, I (Anna) found myself behind the bathroom door of a $600-per-night luxury hotel suite crying profusely about my unexpected sense of overwhelm. The good news is that after fewer than five minutes of alone time I felt much better, splashed and dried my face, and went back out to join the contingent who filled the space throughout the four-day event. The even better news is I have come to realize that moments of retreat like that are available all around me AND that I am in charge of how I feel.

As an only child, I (Nina) appreciated privacy and silence from a very early age. I sometimes wondered if it was weird that I felt uncomfortable in crowds. When I learned Transcendental Meditation I understood that I simply preferred the experience of inward focus and contemplation. Now I understand that retreat is a way to enjoy both: deep inward contemplation in the company of others who enjoy the same.

The purpose of this book is to offer a new way of looking at retreat, to revolutionize the way women define retreat, and to emphasize the power of retreat. Through inspiring weekly reflections, this book demonstrates how you can harness the power of retreat to feel good.

The dictionary defines retreat as "the act of withdrawing, as into safety or privacy; retirement; seclusion." More than that, we say retreat is any time spent withdrawn from the busy-ness of life for the purpose of rest, reawakening, and rejuvenation. Retreat can range from an extra minute in your own bathroom to multiple days in an exotic location, where deep contemplation is intertwined with refreshing experiential interludes that cleanse the physical, emotional and spiritual palettes like cheese and crackers with fine wine.

This book provides 52 mini-retreats—shortcuts to happiness—through reflections of thought. Dip into the deep well of your inner wisdom, drink deeply of your truth, and emerge nourished with new understanding and perspective to enjoy the change and growth you so deeply crave. These 52 reflections are set out to align with the themes and seasons of the calendar year. Each month's theme is thoughtfully paired to an element of our 10 Tips to Release Resistance and Feel Good No Matter What. *See Figure 1.*

Discoveries in retreat feel powerful in the moment. But that's only the spark. The real power of retreat unfolds when you return to routine and gently fan the flame of insight, shifting how you are in circumstances that otherwise remain unchanged. As you nourish and practice newfound awareness, your relationships richen, worry and fear diminish, creativity grows, and satisfaction deepens. As Wayne Dyer says, "Change the way you look at things and the things you look at change."

We so trust the process that together with a small circle of extraordinary friends we engage in a four-day personal retreat twice a year. We so trust the process that we schedule regular retreats to plan and grow our business. We so trust the process that we encourage every woman to find her intimate group, three or four or five whose common purpose is to feel better and better as they move into the next phase of living. Block the time, schedule your location and bring this book to get you started.[1]

There are multiple ways to enjoy this book. You may choose to savor one reflection at a time to set the tone for your week. You may read in order or pick at random. You may look for the entry that speaks to you when you feel

---

1 For a list of potential retreat outcomes see Appendix A.

frustrated, out of sorts, or overwhelmed. Keep a journal or sketchpad at the ready for thoughts and ideas to ponder a specific question or to explore other questions that come up for you. You are in charge! Do what works for you. Have fun with it, and resolve to feel good no matter what!

Wisdom Well Retreats
dip in, drink deep, emerge nourished

www.WisdomWellRetreats.com

Beginning the Journey...
Don't Resist

10 Tips to
Find Relief and
Feel Good No Matter What!

1. Breathe.
2. Don't take yourself too seriously.
3. Don't believe everything you think.
4. Simplify.
5. "No" is a complete sentence.
6. Focus on what you WANT, not on what you don't.
7. Laugh out loud.
8. Take care of yourself first.
9. Choose well.
10. Appreciate!

Info@WisdomWellRetreats.com

Wisdom Well Retreats
dip in, drink deep, emerge nourished

Wisdom Well retreats are among the most useful, high-value events you can experience to release resistance, re-ignite your passion and discover possibility!

It's your turn! Escape from hustle, relax in comfort and explore what's critical to your well-being. Reflect, refocus and re-emerge with processes to feel good no matter what!

Facilitated by Certified Professional Coaches:

Anna Goldsworthy
253-854-3458
anna@WisdomWellRetreats.com

Nina Durfee
425-495-6967
nina@WisdomWellRetreats.com

Figure 1. Our Signature Bookmark

Foreword

Happiness is a choice that requires effort at times.

The Greek dramatist Aeschylus said that, and I guess he should know. Often described as the "father of tragedy," he wrote about large-scale struggles, like the Persian invasion of Greece. He portrayed evil without apology, and yet he had faith that time could heal.

Each of us could tell a tragic story, and yet we know that we are more than our stories. We are conscious beings, and so we have the chance to make a choice.

And so, is Aeschylus correct? Is happiness a choice?

Without denying our struggles with life and ourselves, Anna Goldsworthy and Nina Durfee have teamed up to offer you a "re-treat." That is, you will find tools and reflections within this book to give yourself a treat once again: the choice to feel good.

Retreats are delicious, a fine way to regenerate, and we tend to think they require extensive time and resources. *Feel Good No Matter What* is a gift basket full of mini-retreats that you can enjoy in small increments. The process you'll explore has nothing to do with the meaning of "retreat" that implies defeat or backing away. Instead, you'll have the chance to answer potent questions each week that can move you forward for a lifetime.

Consider this example from week 3: "What am I not looking at?" Good question, right? Because most of us tend to think that with the lens we've been using, we're looking at the whole landscape. In reality, we're only seeing what's contained in the four-sided frame we see through the viewfinder. And what is the human viewfinder? Our mind.

We need to poke our minds to shift from the status quo, to reconnect with what our heart knows. And these questions do just that.

Each month has a theme. You'll begin in January by deciding to resolve to feel good. And then move on to February and loving yourself, which I believe is the key to it all. March brings humor and lightness, and April invites simplicity.

It's a good plan for living the good life: one that is thoughtful, conscious, caring, and purposeful. And you can savor it bit by bit. It's a process, so give yourself permission to take it step by step. That will make it fun instead of overwhelming. And, you'll allow the process to build from the foundation upward and outward—until you feel more expansive, more powerful, more in control of your life.

Even if you aren't as compulsively introspective as I am, you'll find these reflections easy. The whole process is structured for you by two mature, wise, experienced coaches who know firsthand the power of retreat. For these mini-retreats, there's no airfare, no lodging and no uncomfortable floor cushions. Just show up in your jammies with your cup of tea, and you're in.

After feasting on this plan for a year, you might consider one warning: this may lead to something greater! You may, for instance, end up signing up for one of Anna and Nina's longer retreats.

Or then again, you may simply decide that Aeschylus, Nina and Anna are all correct: feeling good no matter what is actually your choice.

Pamela Hale
Author of: *Flying Lessons: How to be the Pilot of Your Own Life*
www.ThroughADifferentLens.com
August, 2013

Introduction

Being happy is the cornerstone of all that you are! You can choose the thought that makes you worry or the thought that makes you happy; the things that thrill you, or the things that worry you. You have the choice in every moment.

Abraham-Hicks

"Feel good no matter what!" We offer this as our mantra not from a place of shallow rainbow platitude but from the deep personal understanding that everyone has the ability to find relief from negativity by opening awareness and shifting perspective. It sounds so simple that it borders on trite or unimportant when, in fact, the power of this concept is formidable.

On September 12, 2001, when the world began to slowly release the collective horror-filled gasp drawn so painfully the day before, I (Anna) was working for the aerospace company that built the planes involved in that mass destruction. Just before my work group convened that day, the company had announced it would lay off 30,000 employees. We were a sad, sorry lot walking into what felt like a room of doom, each of us imagining our own personal tragedy yet to come, when our Project Manager began to speak. "You know," he said, "my experience has been that whenever I have lost a job it has led to something amazing. When I lost my job as a banking executive, my marriage fell apart but I found a new career, and I ended up connecting with the true love of my life."

I realized that I had a similar experience to share: the layoff from my first grown-up job after college also led me directly to marrying the love of my life. One by one, every person in the room added a story of positive transformation that began with a job loss. While not a thing had changed in the world situation, we left the room feeling hope and positive expectation for outcomes that would feel good—no matter what. Our collective vibration of positive energy spiraled upward like a phoenix from the ashes.

According to http://tinybuddha.com/, life isn't good or bad; it just is. Things happen, and we tell ourselves a story. Despite the details that spark it, we can vibrate in a way that feels good, or we can go down in the dumps and feel bad. How we feel is directly related not to the actual event, but to the story in which we wrap it. The familiar Taoist story of the old farmer illustrates this point beautifully. *See Figure 2.*

Science has shown[2] that the words we utter are so powerful they can change the crystalline structure of ice. It follows that what comes out of our mouth or rests in our thoughts has a powerful effect on how we feel. As Shakespeare penned, "Nothing either good or bad, but thinking makes it so."

What's between the covers of this book is not rocket science. It is simply a collection of insights we've accumulated thus far in our self-discovery journeys. It is common sense. It is wonder. It is what has unfolded in our process, individually and together, of reading books, attending workshops, meditating, asking questions, and engaging in coaching and retreat. We came to these reflections by living life, by embracing intense joys, and by surviving heartbreaking challenge.

Shifting from deeply negative emotion to highly positive emotion may not be realistic. What is realistic—even easy— is to focus on a thought, idea, memory, or daydream that feels good when you think about it. This simple small shift helps you release resistance and feel relief right now. Once you've done that, you can do it again and again and again.

2 The Hidden Messages in Water by Masaru Emoto

We are convinced that when you consciously face everyday decisions and choose what feels good and right not because someone else said so but because you know it deep inside, you will unlock your wisdom, ignite your passion, and your soul will dance with joy!

Maybe yes, maybe no

There is a Taoist story of an old farmer who had worked his crops for many years. One day his horse ran away. Upon hearing the news, his neighbors came to visit. "Such bad luck," they said sympathetically.

"Maybe yes, maybe no," the farmer replied. The next morning the horse returned, bringing with it three other wild horses. "How wonderful," the neighbors exclaimed.

"Maybe yes, maybe no," replied the old man. The following day, his son tried to ride one of the untamed horses, was thrown, and broke his leg. The neighbors again came to offer their sympathy on his misfortune. "Maybe yes, maybe no," answered the farmer.

The day after, military officials came to the village to draft young men into the army. Seeing that the son's leg was broken, they passed him by. The neighbors congratulated the farmer on how well things had turned out. "Maybe yes maybe no," said the farmer.

Figure 2 - Taoist Story

January

A New You

*What we call the beginning is often
the end. And to make an end is to make a
beginning. The end is where we start from.*
T.S. Elliot

While many situations in life provide an invitation
to start afresh, none is so universally recognized as the
beginning of a new year. And so we purposefully begin our
retreat adventure in January, the traditional time to focus on
self-assessment and renewal.

This chapter provides five mini-retreat questions
beginning with a vision of how you will feel at the end of this
year and ending with the possibility that you may already
have much of what you seek.

While exploring this chapter, enjoy playing with a more
authentic you and resolve to feel good no matter what!

Tip of the Month:

**Resolve to feel good
no matter what.**

*One of the best ways to make myself happy
is to make other people happy. One of the
best ways to make other people happy is to
be happy myself.*

Gretchen Rubin, *The Happiness Project*

Week 1 - A year from now, will it matter?

At this time of year, many of us take stock of where we are, decide we want something different, and set goals, resolutions, or general intentions to make that happen. As you are creating the new you for the coming year, we invite you to consider how will things be different at the end of the year if you make those changes?

When you resolve to lose 20 pounds, it's not about the number. Connect with what drives you in a way that supports your deeper desire. When you lose 20 pounds, will you feel lighter? More energetic? More capable or confident? The ultimate goal is to feel good. Which feels better: dogged determination to "lose 20 pounds" or imagining feeling light, energetic, and healthy?

Ensure that what you focus on will, in fact, have the impact you seek. Know why you want what you want, and resolve to feel good no matter what!

Week 2 - Does my action advance my purpose?

When we resolve to be different, as is common this time of year, it's easy to forget to think about our bigger desires. How do your resolutions align with what you think you want? When I (Anna) left my corporate job a few years ago, I wrote a letter to myself detailing the post-job life I intended to live. Reading that letter today, I realize that my planned actions were based on the fear of having nothing to do. Acting on that fear-based intention continued the "crazy-busy" life I was trying to leave behind and created frustration that prevented me from realizing my actual intention to stop, smell some roses, and BE more fully with myself and those I love.

When you commit your energy and resources to change, make sure not only that those actions align with what you want in the short term, but be careful that today's focus won't create regrets later on. Resolve to feel good no matter what!

Week 3 - What am I not looking at?

The most obvious truth is often the hardest to see. Think about what you see for others that they don't see for themselves, and be open to the possibility that you are similarly blind to a potential epiphany.

Spend some time this week intentionally observing "you" from a different point of view. Imagine how a friend or even a stranger might perceive your life, and then consider the advice they might provide. Receive that advice with a fresh outlook and an open heart to decide how it might bring great joy or satisfaction your way. Resolve to feel good no matter what!

Week 4 - What do I know for sure?

When looking for sage advice, don't underestimate the value and wisdom that resides within your own heart. No matter your years, all life experiences are filled with a rich education created through each success, failure, and observation of the world around you. Your opportunity for internal learning and growth is infinite.

While Oprah may have a broader range of personal contacts and conversations than most of us, her ability to connect with what she knows for sure is not unique or reserved for the rich and famous. To connect with your own knowing, sit quietly, and allow the answers to come to you. You have the answers, and the more often you ask, the easier they come. Learn to appreciate your well-earned expertise, and resolve to feel good no matter what!

Week 5 - What if I already have it?

Failure to recognize outcome stems from missing the point of your desire.

I (Nina) live in the Pacific Northwest but have a lot of cousins and extended family in New York State. I grew up with the mantra that travel is expensive and "I can't afford it." For years I thought I was doomed never to see my cousins because it was a luxury I couldn't afford. I thought if only I had money, I could fulfill my desire. Then one of my cousins staged a wedding for his son in Seattle, bringing much of the family right to my back yard. I realized then that my financial condition had nothing to do with my ability to enjoy the essence of my desire—family connection.

This week recognize the surprising ways the essence of your desire unfolds. Be present, recognize, and enjoy what you already have. Resolve to feel good no matter what!

February
♡ Love Yourself

*If you aren't good at loving yourself, you will
have a difficult time loving anyone, since you'll
resent the time and energy you give another
person that you aren't even giving to yourself.*
Barbara De Angelis

Whether it's the mothering instinct or some squirrelly
social conditioning, many women tend to put themselves
on hold and take care of everyone else first. Women
come equipped with an overactive responsibility gland
that informs their choices in a way that puts them last.
They defer to the preferences of others. They cater to the
perceived needs of others. They dish up everyone else first
and pick from what's left.

Somehow the notion was engrained that sacrifice is
noble. We're here to tell you otherwise.

The fact is that personal sacrifice wears on the emotions
and deprives you of the very energy and focus you seek to
shine on others. Unless you attend to yourself, out of love for
yourself, you are of little value to others.

Turn the Golden Rule around for a moment. Take time for yourself as you would give it to others. Respect yourself as you would respect others. Love and nourish yourself as you would do for others. Meditate. Take a walk. Play. Laugh. Go on retreat. When your well is dry, you have nothing to give. Replenish and rejuvenate!

February is the month of Love. This month's reflections are designed to help you act out of love for yourself. Employ these tools to feel good and watch the ripple effect encompass an ever-widening circle.

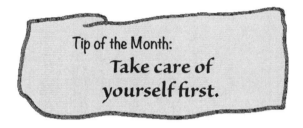

Tip of the Month:
Take care of yourself first.

Don't compromise yourself. You are all you've got.

Janis Joplin

Week 6 - For what will I forgive myself today?

Love knows not blame nor anger nor resentment. Self-love is alignment with the essence of who you really are. Only when you vibrate with the fullness of self-love do you have the capacity to give and receive love from others.

This week, cut yourself some slack and forgive what you consider your weaknesses. Focus instead on your inner and outer strengths. Congratulate yourself for a comment well placed, a job well done, a commitment completed. Take care of yourself first and enjoy the truth of who you are. Resolve to feel good no matter what!

Week 7 - What do I say to myself about myself?

Repeated specific thought about anything—including yourself—strengthens its believability. What does your self-talk say about you? What do you want to believe instead?

This week, be aware of your internal chatter. Does it say you are inadequate, clumsy, forgetful, incapable, or wrong? If you could say something positive about yourself, what would you want to say? Change your self-talk to change your experience. Take care of yourself first by repeating the new statement and watch what unfolds for you. Resolve to feel good no matter what!

Week 8 - Where am I placing my trust?

Do you trust others before you trust yourself? Self-doubt is a time-waster and a distraction. Self-doubt is a roadblock to your truth. When your actions align with your truth, you are self-empowered, and that feels good. When you compromise your truth for another's, you give away your power and close the door to fulfillment.

I (Nina) was faced with a sudden decision to fly cross-country for a family emergency. I felt pinched because (a) I "knew" others expected me to go, (b) last minute airfare was exorbitant, (c) I'd taken time off work the previous week and now, without notice, I was asking for another week off, (d) my day job is part-time, so when I don't work, I don't get paid, which magnified the financial pinch. I felt resentment at being forced into action that felt out of my control. I wanted to dig in my heels and stay, and that felt icky.

My coach asked for my truth. If none of the other factors were present, what would I want to do? My bolt of insight was that if I felt totally free to choose, I would go in a heartbeat.

What made it feel icky was the story I told myself that I was not at choice. When I honored my truth, my decision to travel did not change—how I felt about it changed.

This week, notice when you feel nagged by self-doubt. Close your eyes, take a deep breath, and ask, "What feels true for me?" Trust your gut. Resolve to feel good no matter what!

Week 9 - What am I willing to receive?

Body posture is an indicator of your resistance or your receptivity. Distress over lack of something you want often manifests as physical tension, fatigue, shallow breath, or rapid heart rate. That resistance holds you in a non-receptive state.

This week, when an idea, circumstance, or event seems at odds with something you want, take care of yourself first by noticing your physical stance. When you feel any degree of tension, stand up, lift your gaze, and open your arms wide as if to embrace the entire universe. Notice the release of tension and the automatic expansion of your breath. Say out loud, "I am open and willing to receive what I want." Resolve to feel good no matter what!

March
♡ The Greater You

When you do the common things in life in
an uncommon way, you will command the
attention of the world.
George Washington Carver

March is a month of opposites—in like a lion and out like a lamb. It also celebrates "Everything you think is wrong day" and "Everything you do is right day." This month's retreat questions address the Greater You while encouraging you not to take yourself too seriously.

A case in point: while mounting the stairs to accept her Oscar for Best Actress, Jennifer Lawrence tripped on her elegant designer gown and went down on her knees with her face to the floor. Did her stumble negate her award-winning acting skills? Did it diminish her accomplishment? Did it banish her to obscurity? On the contrary, her ability to laugh and take herself lightly assured her a bigger place in the hearts of her fans and in the memory of the masses.

When it's your turn to mount the platform and accept your Oscar, Nobel Prize, Gold Medal, or Grandmother of the

Century trophy, remember that, despite your footing in the moment, the Greater You and your story are whatever you choose to create—the less seriously the better!

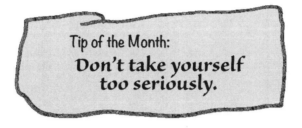

Tip of the Month:
Don't take yourself too seriously.

Life is too important to be taken seriously.

Oscar Wilde

Week 10 - Why do I want what I want?

When you focus solely on what you want without paying attention to why you want it, you are likely not only to pursue the wrong thing but also to block the very thing that you want.

I (Anna) recently told a friend that I want "to spend money without thinking." Even as I spoke, my words surprised me, evoking an image of space filled to the rafters with stuff that doesn't serve me and requires extra daily attention just to manage and store. If I got what I said I wanted, I would sabotage getting what I really wanted, which was...what?

I dug deeper. What I really wanted was to feel different about spending. I wanted to release the feeling of "not enough" and acknowledge that I am always at choice to spend or not. This shift of perspective now allows me to enjoy the conscious choice to not purchase, thereby freeing up space, time, and energy for what truly matters.

This week, when your inner voice says, "I want," challenge yourself to speak that desire out loud. Imagine how you will feel[3] when you have it. Your imagination can evoke that feeling right now. Why depend on something outside of yourself to satisfy your desire? The Greater You already enjoys what you truly want. Don't take yourself too seriously. Resolve to feel good no matter what!

---

3 For help articulating your feelings, see Appendix C.

Week 11 - Where am I stopping short?

When you drive from Seattle to San Francisco, you pass through a lot of territory that is not San Francisco. You don't pull off to the shoulder, lay your head on the steering wheel, and lose faith because you haven't arrived. You stay the course, adjust for construction detours, maybe even change to a more scenic route, but you continue toward your destination.

This week, be aware of discouragement or waning energy for your project or endeavor, and ease up. Don't take yourself too seriously! Remember why you started the journey in the first place. Envision the end result as if it were a destination on the map. Imagine how it will feel to arrive. Remember to enjoy the trip. Re-energize with a rest stop or a snack or a more scenic route, and enjoy what is right now the Greater You. Resolve to feel good no matter what!

Week 12 - What am I afraid of?

At the top of the list of things we fear is failure—but failure of what? One common fear is the failure to meet the expectations of others. Unfortunately, that failure is practically guaranteed—there are so many others and only one of you! Don't take your need to please others so seriously. The Greater You knows that the only expectations that matter are your own.

This week, notice when your fears stem from your assumption of what others might think. Take a deep breath, turn your attention inward, and examine your core values.[4] Trust your own wisdom over that of others, and resolve to feel good no matter what!

4 For help clarifying your values, see Appendix B.

Week 13 - What risk am I willing to take?

Decisions hang on risk. What if it doesn't work? What if I can't? What if so-and-so disapproves? These questions keep us small. Honor the Greater You and consider instead: What if it works? What if it's easy? What if they applaud?

What is it costing you not to take the risk? Is it costing you a sense of accomplishment? Self-esteem? Satisfaction? Stop taking yourself so seriously. If you already don't have it, imagine how you will feel when do. Resolve to feel good no matter what!

April
Spring Cleaning

The ability to simplify means to eliminate the unnecessary so that the necessary may speak.
Hans Hofmann

April's gift is a shift of energy from dormancy to birth and new growth. In preparation for easy growth and natural evolution, our retreat focus this month is to remove that which is no longer necessary. Simplify!

The long winter months provide space for rest, deep contemplation, healing, and rejuvenation. By April that respite has ended; the sun rises earlier each day, and the darkness recedes. Time to awaken!

In the same way daylight expands to dispel the darkness, your time and energy expand as you release what no longer serves you. Follow your urge to clean up and tidy your space, both inside and out. You'll be amazed at how directly your environment affects your energy, drive, and creativity. Tight space and clutter squelch creativity. A simple shift in your physical surroundings opens space and elevates you to new levels of enthusiasm and productivity. Simplify your surroundings!

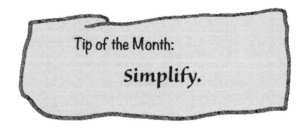

Our life is frittered away by detail.
Simplify, simplify, simplify!

Henry David Thoreau

Week 14 - What am I holding onto?

Spring is a time when new buds break ground, birds sing, and new life springs forth all around. Before the new growth can begin, the old and dead from last year must be allowed to fall away. What are you holding onto right now that is preventing the simple, clean life of your dreams from springing into reality?

We simplify our lives when we release what no longer serves us. Releasing the old creates the opening for new and exciting opportunities. Remove from your closet anything you haven't worn in two years and donate it to charity. Haul away that old ugly chair and bring in something more fitting and beautiful, or simply enjoy the fresh breathing space its absence allows.

This week, when you feel restricted or overwhelmed, calmly consider what you can release or let go of and then breathe into that opening. Take the opportunity to simplify. Resolve to feel good no matter what!

Week 15 - What will make it easy?

"This will be hard. I don't know if I can do this. I'll probably fail anyway, so why try?" When you approach change in this way, the difficulty of your task is assured, and success is seriously jeopardized. What if your desired change was easy? What if creating the ease you desire was as simple as imagining what you want?

Well guess what? Thinking positively requires no more brain power than thinking negatively, and that simple shift in attitude creates an attractive energy that draws you toward an exciting new outcome.

When you feel overwhelmed with anything this week, permit yourself to pause and ask, "What will make this easy?" Take a breath and allow the answer to come. Resolve to feel good no matter what!

Week 16 - What top three values are critical to my well-being?

We live in a crazy-busy culture in the midst of a high-energy world. It's easy to be overwhelmed by all the minutia that fills your waking hours. The key to finding peace in the midst of life's common chaos is to align with your essence, choosing actions, feelings, and thoughts that honor the values you hold dear.

What do you hold dear? It may be security, learning, and trust; or integrity, health, and humor; or excitement, adventure, and commitment; or an infinite number of other options. There are no wrong answers. What is vital is to recognize your values and then consciously allow them into your experience.

Set aside ten minutes to identify and write down the top three values that are critical to your well-being. For some help with this activity go to List of Values in Appendix B as a starting point. Choices that dishonor your values create emotional clutter and distract you from what is critical to your well-being. This week, choose to honor your core values, and Resolve to feel good no matter what!

Week 17 - What am I waiting for?

I (Anna) was almost salivating at the thought of being in the water as I sat beside the pool with my friends on retreat last summer. Suddenly it occurred to me that no one was keeping me from my dream to swim in the pool but me! So I put on my swimsuit and dove in.

How often have you tolerated not having what you want simply because you are used to not having it? Tolerating its absence can become a powerful habit, even when the thing you long for is right beside you. What do you desire that could be yours right now if you simply dove in?

When you find yourself longing for something this week, take a close look at what's keeping you from having it. If it is a matter of habitual thinking, discard that excuse as unneeded clutter. Try on a new thought habit that supports what you want. You may be surprised at how often you discover an opportunity to dive in. What are you waiting for? Stop sitting on the edge, and resolve to feel good no matter what!

Week 18 - What will I let go of today?

Having stuff takes energy. Entertaining thoughts that don't serve you drains energy. Just like clutter on your desk makes your work inefficient, mental clutter can stop productivity in its tracks.

Feeling obligated to my friend, I (Anna) kept her beautiful gift for many years, even after it no longer served me or my space. The friendship was real, but the obligation was imagined. Once I let go of my perceived emotional obligation, I could donate the gift to charity in good conscience. The resulting energy and space were priceless!

This week, notice what's in your space that drains your energy. Is your imagination holding you hostage? What will you let go of in order to enjoy physical and mental clarity? Simplify your life. Resolve to feel good no matter what!

May
♡ Creating You

It is better to create than to learn!
Creating is the essence of life.
Julius Caesar

May is a month of bountiful creation as spring blossoms into summer. What could be cheerier? The natural expression of cheer is laughter, and laughter feels good!

I (Nina) was led to believe that work comes before play. What I now know to be true is when I put play before work, I am more productive and enjoy my work more.

According to an article in *Scientific American*,[5] "On average, watching about 15 minutes of comedy in a group increased pain threshold by 10 percent. Laughing with friends releases feel-good brain chemicals, which also relieve pain."

Robin Dunbar, an evolutionary psychologist at Oxford, reports that it is not the intellectual pleasure of cerebral

5 http://www.scientificamerican.com/article.cfm?id=why-laughter-may-be-the-best-pain-medicine

humor, but the physical act of laughing, the simple muscular exertions involved in producing the familiar ha, ha, ha, that trigger an increase in endorphins, the brain chemicals known for their feel-good effect.[6]

The theory is easy enough to test and really fun to do in your car. Pretend you are a stage actor portraying effusive hilarity. Give the audience a full minute of uproarious belly laughter. How do you feel?

Laughter increases blood flow and oxygen to the brain, stimulating creative juices. Laughter breaks tension. Humor helps us not take ourselves so seriously. Laughter is connection with our core that transcends communication barriers and makes it okay to be who we are. Laughter feels good. Take Nike's advice and just do it!

Oops!

Tip of the Month:

Laugh out loud.

Laugh and be well.

Matthew Green

6 http://www.nytimes.com/2011/09/14/science/14laughter.html?_r=0

Week 19 - Do I choose drudgery, or do I choose fun?

How do you prioritize your to-do list? Doing what feels should invokes weariness, resentment, or a feeling of being overwhelmed. Doing what feels good increases energy, clarity, and productivity. When it comes to conquering your to-do list, saving the best for last fosters neither your greatest productivity nor your deepest satisfaction.

This week, when you eye your to-do list, begin with the task that most boosts your energy. Celebrate its completion with a happy dance and an out-loud laugh, then enjoy the momentum as you check off the rest of your list with greater focus and ease. Resolve to feel good no matter what!

Week 20 - What am I not expressing?

Suppressing ideas, emotions, and passion puts well-being on pause. What creative urge do you squelch in order to take care of "more important" things or the needs of others? Your value to others increases proportionately with your acknowledgment and expression of what is true for you.

This week, push the play button. Loosen your grip on whatever you've been holding in, be it negative emotion or an urge to speak, sing, dance, craft, or engage. Move freely in the wholeness, passion, and joy that expresses the authentic you. Not only will you feel good, but your verve and enthusiasm will be a catalyst for others to waken their creativity as well. Enjoy the win/win, and resolve to feel good no matter what!

Week 21 - What if free and easy were my baseline?

Attitude determines experience. An attitude of worry, blame, or guilt saturates your experience and sets you up for immediate unhappiness.

As a youngster, my (Nina's) son was such a notorious worrier that we nicknamed him Mr. What If. We celebrated his 8th birthday with a roller skating party. Having never been on skates, he was miserable on the ride to the rink as he rattled a continuous litany: "What if I don't know how? What if I fall down? What if they laugh at me?"

We got to the rink and, sure enough, some of those things happened. In spite of that, he eventually found his balance, he had a good time, and at the end of the day he wanted to go again.

My (now adult) son has since learned to feel better in the anticipation of the unknown by changing the direction of his what-ifs. "What if it's easier than it looks? What if it's more fun than I imagine? What if I'm a natural?" And even better: "What if I'm okay with whatever it is?"

This week, set a deliberate intention to release resistance and shift your attitude up a notch to a positive expectation. Find the laughable in every situation. Allow for the possibility of ease and flow, and resolve to feel good no matter what!

Week 22 - What will move me forward with joy?

Faced with an unpleasant task or meeting, do you erect barriers to your own well-being? Barriers may show up as worry, doubt, fear, frustration, or the need to be right. Judgment of others or fear of being judged are also blocks to feeling good. These self-imposed obstacles are no laughing matter.

One of my (Nina's) coaching clients was dreading her evening restaurant work shift with a person she found irritating. She justified her dread: this person had bad manners, he didn't pull his weight, and he was abrasive and uncooperative. My client feared she would react in a way that might jeopardize her own position.

I asked her to imagine how an ideal work night would feel. She said she would feel upbeat, she would get along easily with customers and co-workers, and she would enjoy cooperation and respect. I suggested she evoke that vision prior to setting out for work. She later reported her amazement that by consciously setting her intention, the tone of her whole evening was positive and enjoyable.

This week, preface every meeting, phone call, and personal engagement with an intention to recognize your self-erected barriers, laugh at their irrelevance, and pave the way for release of judgment, worry, and frustration. Allow the possibility for a pleasant—even joyful—encounter. Laugh out loud, practice joy, and resolve to feel good no matter what!

June
Graduation

*Your schooling may be over, but remember
that your education still continues.*
Anonymous

This month, retreating is about breathing into the moment and enjoying the space created by transition. A traditional month of transition, half way through the year, is a second beginning. June is often associated with getting married (the beginning of a journey) or graduating (the completion of a journey in education or career). As children successfully move on to independent endeavors, the resulting empty nest begs the frightening question: "What's my purpose, now that my parenting duties are over?"

It's easy to say that when something ends, a new something is born in its place. But we cannot shift from reverse into drive without going through neutral. It's important to acknowledge, explore, and celebrate the empty space between what has ended and what will come after. Whether it's only a heartbeat of a thought or an extended period of exploration and discovery, the empty space between "what was" and "what will be" is as sacred and precious as the pause between breathing in and breathing out.

If we hang our identity on something that by its very success leaves us out of a job—like being a mother or a teacher or a caregiver—it's no surprise that success is frightening. Living in the moment is the antidote to that fear and the pathway to a new purpose.

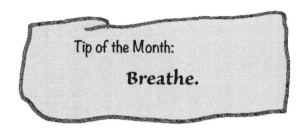

Tip of the Month:

Breathe.

If you want to conquer the anxiety of life, live in the moment, live in the breath.
Amit Ray, *Om Chanting and Meditation*

Week 23 - How do I feel in this moment?

THIS moment right now—the delightfully precious gap tucked between memory and anticipation—is the space where all living happens. Yet we often obliterate it with thoughts of the past or expectation of what is to come.

Granted, life takes some planning to succeed, and savoring special memories feels good too. Still, many of us ignore the present in favor of the past and future more than we realize.

Your thoughts control your feelings, so take a moment right now to assess how you feel. Close your eyes and breathe calmly into your collective body, mind, and spirit. Direct your thoughts to something that feels good. Bask in the good feeling before moving on to the next task. Notice how the good feeling affects what follows.

Throughout the week, be more present "now." Graduate to a more connected relationship with your present feelings. Breathe into the moment, and resolve to feel good no matter what!

Week 24 - How do I find quiet?

According to Oprah, even a minute can make a difference. When you take just a moment to be still, the balance shifts in your favor. Life in our culture seems to be based on the constant uphill accumulation of "more is better" when, in reality, less can be the "more" we're after.

In a world often filled with chaos, what does it take to be quiet? Be creative! Try getting into the car a few moments before takeoff. Close your eyes and sit for a minute or two before turning the key. (Consider working up to five or ten minutes.) Even an extended stay in the bathroom can provide a setting for stillness. What other quiet spaces are waiting to be discovered?

This week, find your quiet space and breathe into the stillness you create. Allow yourself a regular dose, and resolve to feel good no matter what!

Week 25 - How would it feel to let go and trust?

Have you ever bungee-jumped? Or performed a triple gainer off a 10-meter platform? Or surfed Oahu's north shore? Such moves require great trust and a split second of abandon.

While I (Anna) have not taken those plunges, I have said "I do" at the altar (twice to the same guy), left a child with strangers for addiction treatment, and regularly merged into rush-hour traffic. As it turns out, every choice we make requires a certain amount of trust and at least a moment of letting go. Remember that what seems easy for you may be staggering for someone else and vice versa.

This week, remember, acknowledge, and celebrate your major life choices. Ignite the empowerment of trust and letting go. Take a deep breath and imagine applying that same process to whatever causes you fear and hesitation today. Allow a gradual shift, and resolve to feel good no matter what!

Week 26 - What's true for me now?

At age 60 I (Anna) have to admit that middle age is somewhere in my past and I have recently acknowledged entry into the third phase of my life. In doing so, I noticed a major shift in my life trajectory.

The first two-thirds of my life were about creating the future: education (learning about a nest), building a career (funding the nest), finding a partner (to build the nest with), creating a home (feathering the nest), and having a family (filling the nest). I became adept at hunting and gathering to support the growing needs of my nest.

Suddenly (or so it seems) my nest is empty and sits on the sidelines for occasional visitation. It no longer requires expansion, moment-by-moment attention, or my highly honed nesting skills. What a relief!

Just because something has been so for a long time, doesn't make it so now. What shift in your life have you missed or would like to reframe? What freedom are you overlooking in your daily experience? What would it take to create a feeling of graduation with commencement to the next phase of your life?

This week, whether your nest is empty or something else in your life feels lacking, consider shifting your perspective from "empty" to "full of potential." Resolve to feel good no matter what!

July
♡ Being Independent

Never explain. Your friends do not need it
and your enemies will not believe you anyway.
Elbert Hubbard

Our retreat focus this month is independence, so let's be clear what that means. The dictionary definition is "freedom from the control, influence, support, aid, ... of others." Said another way, independence is freedom to let your own core values drive your choices and actions.

When asked for help—and often even when not asked— women in the role of mother, sister, friend, co-worker, or boss often assume the responsibility of tending to the needs of others before their own. They explain, justify, and rationalize to themselves that others' wants and needs come first, and (in their minds) saying "no" would require explanation, justification, or rationalization of their position. It's easier to just say "yes." The truth is, when you do that, you not only neglect your Self, you deprive the other person of the satisfaction that comes from exercising his or her own power of independence.

We're not saying never offer a hand. But decide from a place of (1) nurturing your own core values and well-being and (2) holding others as whole, capable, and resourceful to take care of themselves. Whether you answer "yes" or "no," when your answer supports your core values, it's your right answer.

Engage your power of independence and offer space for others to do the same. Know your truth and don't compromise it. Say "no" out of love for yourself.

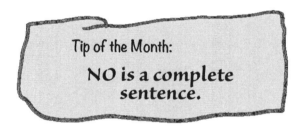

Tip of the Month:

NO is a *complete* sentence.

A 'No' uttered from deepest conviction is better and greater than a 'Yes' merely uttered to please, or what is worse, to avoid trouble.

Mahatma Gandhi

Week 27 - When I say no, what am I saying yes to?

At its simplest, any decision has two sides. What factors guide your choices? Do you forsake what is critical to your own well-being in order to please someone else? If so, do you later feel regret or resentment? Do that often enough and you deplete your own reserves. Then you have nothing to give others.

This week, appreciate each indecisive moment as an opportunity to say "yes" to what is most critical for your well-being. Resolve to feel good no matter what!

Week 28 - What is non-negotiable for me?

Does decision making sometimes feel like bargaining with the devil? When your "yes" is born of guilt or duty or what someone else thinks, you set yourself up for regret. A choice that aligns with your core values feels like ka-chunk— the satisfying mesh of gears into place. Sometimes the only way to ka-chunk is with a solid "no." When I say "no" to an invitation to do an evening presentation, I say "yes" to spending time with my husband and honoring my value of family connection.

This week, notice your moment of choice. Consider if saying "yes" means saying "no" to your non-negotiable core values.[7] Remember, "No" is a complete sentence, with no explanation necessary. Use it purposefully, and resolve to feel good no matter what!

---

7 For help clarifying your values, see Appendix B.

Week 29 - How do my actions support my well-being?

Too much on your plate? Who put it there?

Clutter distracts. Piles of unread catalogs. Abandoned craft projects you plan to resume someday. Email arriving faster than you can read, let alone respond to. Uncluttered space—mental, physical, or electronic—fosters easy breathing, relaxes perceived constraints of time, and supports greater clarity to deliberately choose what's next.

This week, create breathing space by saying "no" three ways: (1) Sweep unread catalogs into the recycle bin and enjoy the beauty of a clean countertop (bonus points if you call the number on the back and ask to discontinue service!). (2) If the craft project doesn't thrill you today, sell it, donate it, or trash it. It's only stuff. If it does thrill you today, stop postponing your joy and play with it! (3) Spend five minutes unsubscribing from emails you keep pushing to the bottom of the pile. Enjoy the expansion of time, expansion of breath, and expansion of beautiful space. Resolve to feel good no matter what!

Week 30 - If I say no, what's the worst that could happen?

The answer to this question depends not on what you are saying "no" to, but on your reason for saying "no." Are you driven by what someone else will think? Are you driven by a standard that someone else has set? If so, a "no" response may set you up for regret or resentment in the long term. The worst case scenario will be a breach of your own integrity. Are you willing to risk that?

This week listen to your gut. What do you know to be true and right for you? Let your truth drive your "yes" or "no" decision, and resolve to feel good no matter what!

Week 31 - I'd rather be _____.

What's the most productive way to fill in this blank? By productive, I mean something that is believable and has a chance for success. Here are three options:

1. Fill in the blank with a condition or circumstance, such as: pretty, rich, healthy or successful. Those don't get you far because (a) they defy concrete definition and (b) there's not much you can do about them right now.

2. Fill in the blank with a status label, such as pilot, auctioneer, mother, dog or president. While some of these are possible, there's a lot of work involved to make it so. Again, not conducive to enjoying the experience right now.

3. Fill in the blank with a feeling, such as optimistic, enthusiastic, mirthful, loving, or passionate. Now there's something you can sink your teeth into! Granted, shifting from deeply negative emotion to highly positive emotion is not realistic. What is realistic—even easy—is to focus on a thought, idea, memory, or daydream that makes you feel good when you think about it. This simple small shift helps you release resistance and feel relief right now. Once you've done that, you can do it again and again and again.

This week, look at negative emotion as an opportunity to practice feeling relief. This is the essence of retreat—to deliberately let go of resistance and allow yourself to feel good. Say "no" to resistance, and resolve to feel good no matter what!

August
💗 Relax and Rejuvenate

*Everything you do can be done better
from a place of relaxation.*
Stephen C. Paul

August (at least in the northern hemisphere) is traditionally a time for vacation, for getting away, for relaxing and refreshing. But how many times have you returned from vacation to bigger piles and to-do lists than were there before you left?

When you are deprived of a healthy ongoing balance of work and play, vacation becomes a time to push beyond your comfort zone, overtax your budget, and even cross the line of dignified behavior in the name of recovery from a year spent nose-to-the-grindstone, doing what's right, and being a good example. Frankly, vacations frequently defeat their very purpose.

The good news is that by regularly allowing yourself small interludes to relax, reflect, and rejuvenate, you can be focused and intentional on vacation, knowing it's not an all-or-nothing affair.

This month's reflections focus on the all-important topics of why you want what you want and releasing the self-imposed thoughts of failure that stand between you and your dreams. We invite you to relax, rejuvenate, and direct your focus to what you want.

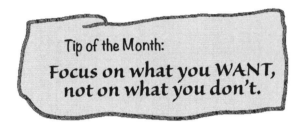

Tip of the Month:

Focus on what you WANT, not on what you don't.

Whether you think you can or think you can't, either way you are right.

Henry Ford

Week 32 – What is my personal mission statement?

A personal mission statement defines your reason for existence. If you don't know where you are going, how will you know when you get there? When you desire to live your life on purpose, creating or knowing your purpose is an essential first step.

Here are some sample mission statements:

- From Amazon: "Our vision is to be earth's most customer centric company; to build a place where people can come to find and discover anything they might want to buy online."
- From Nike: "To bring inspiration and innovation to every athlete in the world."
- I believe everything happens for a reason, and there is no better place to be than right here, right now.
- I am guided by my values and beliefs, to give thanks in some measurable way, and to laugh out loud every day.
- I respect myself and others.
- I find something to appreciate about everyone I meet.

Think about what draws you in and forget about the imagined barriers that might block the way. This week, pay attention to what feels authentic for you, and write a sentence or two summarizing your own reason for existence. Keep it fresh in your mind and notice how often circumstances fall into place to make it so.

Focus on what you want, and resolve to feel good no matter what!

Week 33 - What do I want more of in my life?

We often focus on what is wrong about our lives and ourselves so we can work to make things better. We are told to strengthen our weaknesses to be more balanced. Unfortunately, focusing on weakness or on what doesn't work minimizes the power of our strengths and actually attracts more of exactly what we do not want.

In fact, we are surrounded every day by good things and delightful choices. What would make you feel better? Is it more family time, a creative activity, time in the water, or simply an afternoon power nap? What is it costing you to deprive yourself of that?

This week, conjure the feeling of having what you want. Don't be surprised when you begin to notice more of the good stuff showing up everywhere you look. Focus on what you DO want, and resolve to feel good no matter what!

Week 34 - What energizes me?

When I (Anna) make my mother-in-law's famous Crazy Cake recipe, magic happens! Adding vinegar to the dry flour mix that contains the baking powder causes an eruption of energy and the promise of a cake that will rise. It doesn't matter how long the pan of dull, lifeless powder sits in waiting, the combination reacts immediately every time. The resulting cake is always inspiring and delicious!

Our lives are like that cake mix in waiting. We each have elements that spark energy and enthusiasm to the core of our being. Paying attention only to the basics of day-to-day experience is an acceptance of life as dull and uninspiring, when adding a small amount of your key ingredient can ignite passion and raise you to new heights.

This week consider, "What is the vinegar to my baking powder?" Relax and allow a small measure of your favorite ingredient to rejuvenate your being. Focus on what you want, and resolve to feel good no matter what!

Week 35 - What would I do if I knew I couldn't fail?

The old saying goes, "The only real failure in life is the failure to try." Most of the time it's not something real, but the fear of an imagined failure that paralyzes us.

According to Nexus, Colorado's holistic journal,[8] guided imagery "is used to promote physical, mental and emotional health by imagining positive images and desired outcomes to specific situations. Visualization therapy is believed to encourage activity in the right hemisphere of the brain, related to creativity and emotions." Visualization is even used as an adjunct to conventional cancer treatment!

Since failure is not an option, what experience will you visualize? How big will you dream? This week relax, dream big, and allow your guided imagination to attract your most outrageous desires. Resolve to feel good no matter what!

---

8 http://nexuspub.com/altmed/tools/visual.htm

September
Back to School

Learning to live is learning to let go.
Sogyal Rimpoche

I (Nina) love the back-to-school promise of infinite possibility: a fresh pad of paper, sharp pencils, a world of knowledge to explore and drink in! This month's retreat is about where to focus next, what to learn, which friends to reconnect with, and which new people to invite to the experience. Decisions, decisions! So many choices to make in the course of a day, a year, a lifetime. What drives your choices?

It's been said that "not deciding" equals "deciding not." I disagree. Not deciding binds you in a sort of limbo that renders you a victim of uncertainty. There is power in conscious decision, and when you put off deciding, you turn away from your power. When you put off decision, you stay stuck in the log jam of immobility. When you decide, even if you "decide not," you break away from the log jam and get back into the free flow of forward motion.

When you opt to "not decide," you live by default. When you "decide" or "decide not," you live by design.

But what if you don't know what to decide? Get quiet for a moment, take a deep breath, put your attention on one option at a time, and notice how you feel. Does this choice energize you or zap your strength? Does it thrill you or bore you? Do you love it or does it leave you flat? Trust your heart and trust your instinct. Free yourself from the log jam of indecision, choose deliberately, and enjoy the unfolding of what's next for you.

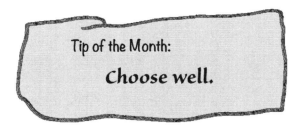

Tip of the Month:

Choose well.

Everyone should carefully observe which way his heart draws him, and then choose that way with all his strength.

Hasidic saying

Week 36 - What am I waiting for?

What would you love to do but continue to put off until "later?" Enjoy a play day with your best friend? Take a pottery class? Walk on the beach? Sky dive? How do you define "later?" After you clean the house? After you pay off the car? After the kids leave home? When you retire?

Whoever said "life is not a dress rehearsal" had it spot on. Life is right here, right now. Every moment of every day you are at choice about what you do next. When you defer joy, you suffocate spirituality. Which epitaph do you want: "She was disciplined" or "She enjoyed life to the fullest"?

This week, notice the moments when you put yourself on hold. What is it costing you to defer joy? Choose well, and resolve to feel good no matter what!

Week 37 - Where am I willing to stretch?

As a new student of the potter's wheel, I (Nina) am learning the importance of centering the clay. When the clay is not centered, it wobbles, loses integrity, and collapses in on itself. The first few times this happened, I felt frustrated and inept. Then I watched a pottery demonstration by D. Cuzick, who intentionally stretched the clay to the point of collapse and allowed the sides of his bowl to fold inward and lie limp.

Rather than interpreting collapse as failure, he offered a surprising new perspective. He turned the bowl upside down and allowed the walls to come off the inside, hanging down kind of curvy. He set the bowl to dry overnight in the inverted position. Next day he had a bowl with a unique undulated shape, not only useful, but beautiful and ready to glaze and display.

How is clay a metaphor for your life? What stretch or flop have you feared? What new truth might surprise you when you take that stretch or view the flop from a different perspective?

This week, embrace the breakdown of failure that allows the breakthrough to unexpected success. Stretch the mold, and resolve to feel good no matter what!

Week 38 - What does my gut tell me?

Emotional discomfort is a great tool. That queasy feeling you get whenever you think, "I should be such-and-such," or "they expect me to do that and I don't want to," or "what I do won't be good enough," indicates misalignment between the story you tell yourself and what is really true for you. Right or wrong is not the issue. The issue is your trust or mistrust in the validity of your own knowledge or desire.

This week, instead of whining about the pain of your clenched stomach, acknowledge its significance. Take the cue to examine what you really think, know, and want. Grant yourself permission to trust your gut. Choose well. Act in a way that supports your values, your truth, and your well-being. Resolve to feel good no matter what!

Week 39 - What action would serve me better?

Feeling bored? Mired in the same old grind? Tired of the same underwhelming result? You've no doubt heard the adage, "Keep doing what you're doing and you'll keep getting what you're getting." Habits are a great tool to maximize efficiency. But what was useful two years ago may not be useful now.

Changing a habit of thought, speech, or assumption ("it takes money to make money," "I never remember names," "aging is painful and ugly") can be a challenge. But even a change as simple as putting on the other sock first, stirring your coffee with the other hand, or taking a different route to work triggers the neurons in the brain to fire differently. This small physiological change stimulates new pathways in the brain, alters perspective, and leads to recognition of opportunities and solutions that you may not have seen before.

This week, question the effectiveness of your engrained habits. Mix it up, change something small, and watch what happens. Resolve to feel good no matter what!

October
♡ Skeletons in the Closet

*You get to an age where you get tired of
hiding behind whatever people think is correct.*

Betty Wright

October is the month of Halloween—ghosts, goblins,
and skeletons! This month's reflections focus on liberating
yourself from the skeletons that lurk in your mental closet,
holding you scared and powerless.

I (Nina) stole this month's tip ("don't believe everything
you think") from a bumper sticker. It made me laugh, and it
made me think.

Thoughts you think over and over become your beliefs.
Thoughts and beliefs drive action, and action generates
outcome. What thoughts have you harbored for decades that
drive the actions that produce results that fall short of what
you want?

Shad Helmstetter, author of What to Say When You
Talk to Your Self, claims, "The longer you have bought the

thought, the truer it is." Do thoughts like these lurk in your subconscious:

- 💜 The older I get the less energy I have.
- 💜 I can't afford it.
- 💜 I'm directionally challenged.
- 💜 I don't have enough time.
- 💜 I'm horrible with names.

Mental or verbal repetition of thoughts makes them your truth. What truth do you want instead?

Release your old, worn out beliefs to the light of day, and clear space for friendlier truths. Take charge of your beliefs, and resolve to feel good no matter what!

Tip of the Month:
Don't believe everything you think.

Often the opposite of a great truth is also true.

Gretchen Rubin

Week 40 - What assumptions do I make?

A skeleton is a framework to support a predictable form. How we experience our actions, conversations, and relationships depends on our framework of beliefs and assumptions. The longer we've assumed something, the more fully it fleshes out the framework of our experience. We get what we expect.

Two people sit side by side on a trans-Atlantic flight. One calmly does a puzzle, reads a book, or talks easily about her upcoming vacation. The other is afraid of flying. Her heart flutters erratically. Sweat oozes from her palms and her upper lip. Her stomach cramps in pain. Circumstances are the same for each of them, but they have different experiences based on their beliefs or assumptions.

Assumptions of unworthiness and unlovability form the skeleton (framework) that supports negative experience. What skeletons are in your closet?

This week, notice your negative and positive experiences. Identify and question the assumptions that form the basis of your negative experience. Release the beliefs that stifle well-being, and resolve to feel good no matter what!

Week 41 - What am I pretending not to know?

Pretense disconnects us from who we really are. We concoct plenty of reasons not to express and act on our own strength, power, and wisdom. Pretending not to know relieves us from the duty of performing and potentially failing. Deferring to another reduces our risk of being blamed. It lets us off the hook and allows us to avoid embarrassment.

The off-the-hook comfort of knowing you won't be blamed is a pretense that disempowers you. Pretending not to know dismantles the very framework (skeleton) that supports your well-being.

This week, dare to release the skeleton (your wise inner voice) from your closet. When the old habit of self-doubt bubbles up, acknowledge it, question it, and step into what is true for you. Life lived from a place of authenticity and integrity is rich and rewarding. Engage the power of your inner wisdom, and resolve to feel good no matter what!

Week 42 - How does this thought serve me?

A woman rubs at a dark spot on her leg (curiously observing what is and trying to change it). It won't come off. "It must be a spider vein," she says with dismay. (Assumption) "And it's ugly!" (Judgment) "Don't you think it's ugly?" (Gathering support for self-judgment) "What do you think it is?" (Focusing more intently on what she does not want) "I hate this!" (Anger) "My mother had these and now I'm getting them." (Resentment, hopelessness) "I hate getting old!" (Powerlessness) "This is embarrassing." (My happiness depends on what others think) "I'll never wear shorts again." (Bondage) "I'm going to try one more time to scrub it off." (Desperation)

Focusing on what is wrong or "imperfect," however true it is, magnifies its presence. When we fill the movie screen of our awareness with what is not working, we obliterate the space for what we want instead.

It's not that you should deny what is. But continued focus on anything, no matter how "true" it is, makes it more dominant in your experience. What focus will serve you better?

The good news is you don't have to resort to empty Pollyanna platitudes. Simply shift your attention to another person, thing, or circumstance that makes you feel better when you think about it. Whatever was dragging you down will fade into the background. The positivity of your new focus will dominate the screen, and you will feel better. Right now. *(PS: The spot washed off. The downward spiral of negative feelings was created solely in her thoughts.)*

This week, question the value of thoughts, feelings, and that feel bad when you think them. Shift your attention to anything that feels better: someone you love, the antics of your pet, an exhilarating or peaceful experience. Resolve to feel good no matter what!

Week 43 - What's another perspective?

We've entered the delightful age of repurposing. Bath mats out of wine corks, advent calendars out of old Christmas cards, wind chimes out of Grandma's silverware.

When my (Nina's) pottery pieces come out of the kiln cracked or broken, I tuck them away in my garden for added color and texture. It shifts my focus from failure to creativity.

What makes you unhappy when you focus on it? Your husband's tardiness? Your co-worker's eating habits? Your economic outlook? Negative emotion stems from looking at what you do not want. What shift of perspective will ease your attitude?

Don't try to cram a square peg into a round hole. In other words don't wrack your brain to remember when your mate was on time, thinking that will make you happy. Instead look for a "round peg"—something you truly appreciate about him: the way he fills your coffee cup without being asked; the things he says that make you giggle.

This week, repurpose your negative perspective by using it as a launching pad to something better. Resolve to feel good no matter what!

Week 44 - If no one would object, what would I stop, start, or continue?

When I (Nina) began tinkering with this question, I thought I would be writing about the irrelevance of what others think when it comes to our own well-being. But that didn't resonate for me, and I kept re-starting. Finally, I thought what better way to get a handle on this than to write my own list of things I would do if no one would object. Surely it would expose that other bugger who gets in my way.

Boy did I have a wrong number!

I listed some things I would do "if no one would object." Spend more time at the pottery shop. Learn to play the blues. Empty my closet and start from scratch. Hire a housekeeper. See more stage plays.

Bolt of insight: no one else objects to any of this! I'm the one who deprives myself of these pleasures using the lame excuses that I don't have enough time, it costs too much, it's pretentious, I'm not worthy, or it's frivolous and unproductive. I'm the one who puts these labels on all of it. I'm the one who's been objecting all along!

The good news is, now I know. Now I can explore ways to release my sense of unworthiness, my sense that there is a shortage of time or money. Most importantly, I can work on clarifying my own personal values and set about prioritizing for the sake of my own well-being. (Hint: working with a coach speeds up this process considerably!)

This week, examine your truth. Question the belief that someone else's objection or expectation keeps you stuck. Accept your capacity to deny or allow the life you love. Don't believe everything you think. Honor your core values, and resolve to feel good no matter what!

November
Your Bountiful Harvest

*Acknowledging the good that is already in
your life is the foundation for all abundance.*
Eckhart Tolle

What follows more naturally from bountiful harvest
than Thanksgiving—a time to appreciate what was and what
now lies before us. The dictionary defines appreciation as
"gratitude; thankful recognition." For the purpose of retreat,
I suggest appreciation is much more than the dictionary
definition.

The act of appreciating creates a welling up of love
from the heart. It is a knowing felt in the solar plexus.
Appreciation is warmth radiating from the inside outward—
not like a hot flash, but like a warm, safe, loving essence,
a knowing that all is well and perfect even in its perceived
imperfection. Appreciation is not just the recognition but
the experience of the Divine in all things.

What you focus your attention on grows stronger.
Appreciation for any aspect of a person, thing, or event

engages the very molecules of goodness. Every time you appreciate, you plant a seed that, nurtured with attention, blossoms in ultimate beauty and fruition, and produces seeds to create more.

Appreciation perpetuates fulfillment.

Tip of the Month:

Appreciate.

Gratitude unlocks the fullness of life. It turns what we have into enough, and more. It turns denial into acceptance, chaos to order, confusion to clarity. It can turn a meal into a feast, a house into a home, a stranger into a friend.

Melody Beattie

Week 45 - What do I most appreciate about myself?

In my (Nina's) book, *Full Bloom: 7 Practical Steps to Get What You Want +1 to Grow On*, I name appreciation as the "1 to Grow On" step that perpetuates the process of satisfaction and fulfillment. How exactly does that work?

You attract what you think about, whether you want it or not. Attention to what feels like your shortcomings not only brings your own "shortcomings" into clearer focus, it also fosters your awareness of the shortcomings of others. Acknowledgment of your strengths, your wisdom, and your creativity unveils a buffet of possibility. Self-appreciation enhances your ability to perceive the worthiness, creativity, and wisdom of others.

This week, focus consciously on your positive qualities. Love yourself, appreciate yourself, and resolve to feel good no matter what!

Week 46 - What ignites my passion?

Many a client has said to me (Nina), "If I only knew what my passion was, I would follow it." This assumes "passion" to mean a calling to do something specific, like flying spaceships or carving statues or feeding the hungry. In fact, "passion" refers not to action but to the feeling it generates. Passion, according to Webster, is "boundless enthusiasm, a concept that denotes fervor, ardor, and zeal."

You may feel passionate about going to New York, but that doesn't make New York your passion. Passion is your reason for choosing New York. Maybe you are drawn to the architecture. Or someone lives there whose company you enjoy. Or Broadway musicals thrill you. Or you want a change of scenery.

Passion comes not from New York but from the feeling it evokes for you: expanded knowledge or understanding; rich, personal connection; the infusion of joy and energy from live song and dance; or the spiritual freedom of cross-country travel.

Appreciation for what feels good enlivens passion in all that you do. This week, act to enliven your senses and your soul. Appreciate, live passionately, and resolve to feel good no matter what!

Week 47 - What influence has made the greatest impact on my life?

Appreciation for positive influences is easy. Loving parents, close friends, teachers who believed in you—what's not to love?

But what about the "negative" influences? How were you affected by your encounter with the bully, the loss of a loved one, the falling stock market, or bad news from the doctor?

At first blush you may be inclined to resent those people and events for the pain you felt. But what if those "negative" influences offer a platform to strengthen, adapt, and perform in ways you otherwise might not have achieved?

For years I (Nina) envied friends and family who knew the security, comfort, and consistency of growing up together in the same community, developing deep, rich roots and relationships. As an Air Force brat, I was uprooted every couple of years to a new city or state. I envied the permanence of long-term roots, familiar faces, and predictable routines.

Now when I return to the places I thought I'd never wanted to leave, they look different to me. The people seem not to have changed much—something I appreciate but also something I don't relate to. My exposure to a wider piece of the world has shifted my physical and social perspective. Where once I longed for permanence, now I understand that change is a fundamental characteristic of all of life. Permanence, almost by definition, denies change and stagnates growth. This understanding gives me new appreciation for both "positive" and "negative" experiences.

This week, explore what has felt like negative influence on your life with an intention to shift your perspective and understanding, and resolve to feel good no matter what!

Week 48 - How do I express appreciation?

Don't you love the feeling of being recognized, acknowledged, and appreciated? It comes in so many ways: a smile or nod; someone remembers your name; buys you coffee; says thank you; lets you merge into traffic; holds the door for you; pats you on the back; listens attentively; makes you the focus of conversation; respects your opinion, though it differs from theirs; clears the table; bags your groceries; compliments your skill or talent; makes time for you.

As surely as those things feel good to you, they feel good to others as well. And when you genuinely appreciate another, you expand your own capacity for love and joyfulness.

This week, pick a number from 10 to 20. Challenge yourself to actively express appreciation in that many different ways to that many different people, especially when you are feeling annoyed or disrespected or unappreciated. Notice how you feel each time you shift from "poor me" to authentic appreciation of someone or something else. Enjoy the empowerment of appreciation, and resolve to feel good no matter what!

December
♡ Celebrating You

The applause is a celebration not only of the
actors but also of the audience. It constitutes
a shared moment of delight.
John Charles Polanyi

December heralds the season associated with joy, celebration, and giving. For many women, it also heralds a season of pure physical and mental exhaustion.

We believe that retreat is a withdrawal from the "busy-ness" of life for the purpose of rest, reawakening, and rejuvenation.

In contrast to the outside world, the focus for this month is simple and low-key. Set aside a few minutes each day to retreat, breathe, and release your resistance to taking care of yourself.

Celebrate You as you absorb the joy of the season and you will notice many shared moments of delight. Resolve to enjoy all the seasons of your life.

Tip of the Month:

Don't resist.

Resistance is thought transformed into feeling. Change the thought that creates the resistance, and there is no more resistance.

Robert Conklin

Week 49 - What's the hurry?

Ready, fire, aim! Never a good plan for a pleasing outcome.

Whose idea was this hectic chaos anyway? Having kicked off sometime mid-year, the crazy-busy holiday season is approaching full speed. Do you feel overwhelmed with options, over-scheduled with obligations, and at least a little under-funded for the huge responsibility our surrounding culture has come to inspire and the media to promote?

What if you had a plan to suit your comfort level, your schedule AND your budget? If you don't do it intentionally, the schedule and the budget will direct choices through chance and random happenstance not necessarily in your best interest.

While the main event is still a few weeks away, consciously set a window of time to engage a slow down. Schedule a daily personal retreat to review what's on your plate and identify what will best energize, sustain, and fulfill you. Release the urge to stuff yourself with "dutiful" activity. Do what feels good, and walk away from the rest without regret.

Don't stuff yourself to the bursting point. Instead, enjoy an intentional sampling of the delights of the season. Resolve to feel good no matter what!

Week 50 - What's the best gift I can give myself?

What if the best thing you can give yourself is also the best for everyone else?

As the holidays set in I (Anna) often find myself so wrapped up in taking care of others that I don't put myself on the list at all, let alone at the top. Loved ones watching me might assume that to be on my team, you must work until it hurts and hold self-sacrifice above all else. OMG!!

Instead, I want my granddaughters to see that Grandma has fun and puts people (herself included) above stuff, things, and arbitrary schedules. The most important gift I can give is to model that life is fun and that there is always "enough."

This year, consider making yourself the primary gift under the tree, and notice the joy of those you love when they delight in being with you instead of watching you do yourself in for them!

Enjoy yourself and those you love this holiday season. Don't resist the urge to feel good!

Week 51 - Happy Holidays!

The holiday is here. What will allow you to be present for it?

Focus on that, and resolve to feel good no matter what!

Week 52 - What feels good right now?

Year's end is a traditional time to reflect, review, and refocus. Before bursting into the New Year, take a moment to enjoy a cup of tea or a glass of wine and review the mini-retreats you've indulged in during this year. What surprised you? What insights have you gained? How are you different? What do you know for sure? What else do you want to celebrate?

Think of this week as the neutral space between the waning year and the year about to be born. Before kicking off the upcoming year of opportunity and possibility, bask in the celebration of YOU.

Don't resist what feels good right now. Resolve to feel good no matter what!

Epilogue
♡ Anticipation

Oh the places you'll go! There is fun to be done! There are points to be scored. There are games to be won. And the magical things you can do with that ball will make you the winning-est winner of all.

Dr. Seuss, *Oh, the Places You'll Go!*

And the cycle of life continues...

Tip of the Month:
**Dip in, drink deep,
emerge nourished.**

What am I excitedly anticipating?

Fireworks on the 4th of July, a party for my (Anna's) birthday, the hip replacement that remobilized me, the birth of each of my granddaughters—those were events scheduled into my life that created excitement and anticipation.

As the New Year approaches once again, we are primed to look forward to what will pass through the coming year. What if you approached each day with the same eager excitement and anticipation as imagining the next year?

For the first week of the New Year, intentionally begin each day in conscious, eager anticipation. At the end of the week, review how it felt and decide how you want to feel the week after that and the week after that. Be happy, be healthy, be prosperous, be good to yourself, and resolve to feel good no matter what!

Appendix

Appendix A · Potential Retreat Outcomes

Extended retreat is the perfect space for releasing the baggage of guilt, arrogance, and false humility so that you can authentically and wholly know and appreciate your true Self.

Women who participate in Wisdom Well Retreats with Anna and Nina report profound shifts in experience. Not only do they find the retreat itself to be a deeply enjoyable experience, they also report effects that last long after they have returned to their busy schedules. Among the results reported by retreat attendees are:

- ♥ I find relief from feeling overwhelmed
- ♥ I reflect, reframe, refocus
- ♥ I get unstuck
- ♥ I rekindle my passion
- ♥ I gain a new perspective
- ♥ I learn how to feel good no matter what
- ♥ I discover possibility
- ♥ I relax in a comfy, secluded setting
- ♥ I enjoy deep connection and camaraderie with women who "get" me
- ♥ I feel safe
- ♥ I am heard without being judged
- ♥ I am challenged to question my habits of thought
- ♥ I gain clarity and direction
- ♥ I feel good about being authentically and unapologetically me
- ♥ I do less and accomplish more
- ♥ I feel an increase in confidence
- ♥ I am re-energized
- ♥ I like myself better

If you'd prefer a guided experience, Anna and Nina offer the option of extended retreat over three to four days where you benefit from professional coaching expertise both individually and as a group. To inquire about a retreat for your group, visit www.WisdomWellRetreats.com.

Appendix B · Values

What are values? Values are qualities of intrinsic worth, a reflection of your essential self, the center of your being where what matters most to you is known.

Why do values matter? Acknowledging your values and honoring those values through your choices and decisions impacts the quality of your life. Clarifying your values and thoughtfully using those values to guide your choices and decisions can be an ongoing process. When you fully incorporate a values-based approach to life, you will experience greater purpose, feel more fulfilled, and manifest your desires with greater ease.

Values are related to, but not the same as, morals and ethics. A moral is a philosophical principle of right and wrong. Ethics are a system of moral standards.

Each person has his or her unique priority for personal values, and whether consciously adopted or unconsciously inherited, they become habits. While people tend to feel quite strongly about these qualities, values are neither positive nor negative, nor are they good or bad. They do, however, have a profound influence on an individual's quality of life.

Identify your own list of values:

- ♥ Carefully read through the columns of words that follow, and circle or highlight any that feel particularly important to you.
- ♥ Identify your top twelve values.
- ♥ Select the top three that feel of most critical importance to your well-being.

List of Values

abundance
accomplishment
accountability
accuracy
achievement
acknowledgment
adventure
aesthetics
authenticity
balance
beauty
celebration
change
choice
cleanliness
collaboration
communication
community
completion
comradeship
connectedness
connection
consistency
contribution
creativity
direction
diversity
economic use
education
elegance
empowerment
encouragement
energy
excellence

excitement
expansion
exploration
expression
flexibility
focus
forgiveness
freedom
fulfillment
growth
harmony
honesty
honor
humility
humor
independence
integrity
joy
justice
laughter
lightness
liveliness
love
luxury
nourishment
nurturing
orderliness
participation
partnership
peacefulness
peaceful
coexistence
perfection
performance

personal power
productivity
prosperity
punctuality
recognition
relaxation
reliability
risk taking
romance
routine
safety
security
serenity
service
silence
simplicity
sincerity
space
spirituality
spontaneity
success
support
teamwork
thrift
to be known
tolerance
tradition
trust
truth
validation
vitality
warmth
wisdom
zest

Appendix C · Feelings

Feelings are a precise indicator in the moment of how aligned you are with your values. When you feel good you are well aligned. When you feel less than good, it's a clear signal that you are out of alignment with the values you hold dear. It's as simple as that.

Feelings are an expression of what's going on in your subconscious mind. What you say and how you say it impacts how you feel. Identifying how you feel at a conscious level is the first step to changing a negative experience or maintaining and enhancing a positive one.

To help you articulate why you'd like to change something (a person, circumstance, or condition), we offer the list of Negative Feelings. To help you articulate what you want to feel instead, we offer the list of Positive Feelings. We recommend that you not spend too much time on the Negative Feelings list – after all, you get what you think about!

Once you specify what you don't want, find what you're reaching for on the Positive Feelings list. We encourage you to daydream (for a minute or an hour or a day) how that positive emotion feels. Conjure it in your body, feel it in your heart, imagine the experience you desire. Have fun with it!

Positive Feelings

absorbed
adequate
affectionate
aggressive
amused
appealing
ardent
avid
blissful
bold
brave
brisk
buoyant
calm
carefree
celebrate
cheerful
cheery
cherish
close
comfortable
competent
complacent
concerned
confident
content
courageous
creative
curious
daring
dashing
determined
eager
earnest
ease
ecstatic
elated
elegant
eloquent
encouraged
energized
engrossed

enjoy
enriched
enthusiastic
excited
exhilarated
fascinated
fearless
festive
fine
free
frisky
fulfilled
fun
generous
giddy
glad
glorious
grateful
gratified
happy
hardy
heroic
hilarious
humorous
impulsive
independent
inquiring
inquisitive
inspired
intentional
interested
intrigued
jolly
joyful
jubilant
keen
lighthearted
loving
loyal
merry
mindful
open

optimistic
overjoyed
passionate
peaceful
playful
pleased
poignant
proud
reassured
refreshed
rejuvenated
relaxed
relief
relish
renewed
restful
satisfied
savor
secure
seductive
serene
sexy
silly
sincere
soft
sparkling
spirited
superb
surprised
tender
thrilled
vibrant
vital
vivacious
warm
witty
wise
worthy
zany
zesty

Negative Feelings

Accusatory
Agitated
Alone
Angry
Anxious
Apathetic
Arrogant
Ashamed
Bored
Cheated
Clammy
Close-minded
Clumsy
Confined
Cowardly
Dependent
Depleted
Depressed
Despair
Devastated
Dim
Disappointed
Discouraged
Dispirited
Displeased
Disrespected
Distant
Distaste
Distracted
Doltish
Doubtful
Drained
Dread
Dull
Dumpy
Embarrassed
Empty
Envious
Fearful
Foggy

Fragmented
Frail
Frumpy
Frustrated
Glum
Greedy
Guilty
Hard
Heavy
Hopeless
Hurt
Impatient
Inadequate
Incompetent
Indecisive
Ineffective
Inexperienced
Insecure
Insincere
Intolerant
Irritated
Jealous
Lackluster
Lethargic
Low
Lustful
Mad
Mediocre
Murderous
Naive
Negative
Overwhelmed
Overworked
Pessimistic
Powerless
Queasy
Reluctant
Repulsive
Resigned
Restricted

Rigid
Rough
Sad
Scared
Scattered
Selfish
Separate
Shocked
Sickly
Sluggish
Sour
Spiteful
Squeamish
Stagnant
Stale
Stingy
Stinky
Stuck
Stunted
Stupid
Tense
Tight
Timid
Tired
Trapped
Unattractive
Unclear
Underappreciated
Undeserving
Unenthused
Unfocused
Unhappy
Unqualified
Untrustworthy
Unwanted
Unworthy
Vengeful
Weak
Worried
Zapped

About the Authors

The Retreat Ladies, Anna Goldsworthy and Nina Durfee, have both experienced putting themselves on hold while juggling a marriage of 30+ years, raising boys, engaging professionally in the corporate world, and transitioning to encore careers. Each dabbles playfully in artistic creation, Anna with beads, paper and paint and Nina with pottery. Each has agonized as her son named Jake navigated extreme substance abuse through teen and early adulthood. Each has gratefully experienced the joy of her Jake emerging as a loving husband and father with a successful and gratifying career. But there the similarities end.

Nina[9] and Anna[10] are nearly polar opposites in their preferences, structure, and modus operandi:

Nina	Anna
Morning	Evening
Paper	Electronic
Action	Thought
Words	Pictures
Content	Container
Petite	Statuesque
Verbal processor	Silent processor
Bottom line	More data
Simplicity	Complexity
Grandsons	Granddaughters
Only child	Three siblings
Transitory	Rooted
Outdoors	Indoors

9 Nina's photo by Tammy Hunter
10 Anna's photo by Simply Stated Photography

Together, Certified Professional Coaches Anna and Nina have over 7000 hours of coaching and retreat experience. They established Wisdom Well Retreats because they believe in the powerful benefits of retreat. Their critical balance and full spectrum of viewpoint and understanding offer broad value for their retreat participants.

Anna and Nina empower empty nested career women to tame their overactive responsibility glands and reconnect with joy and passion. They combine passion and commitment with their wisdom and good humor to create a cozy, soul-feeding atmosphere that allows you to be authentically, joyfully, and unapologetically you!

Visit them online at www.WisdomWellRetreats.com.

Nina Durfee

I first met with a coach when I was desperate to make a change and thought I was out of options. I know the fragility of wanting something bigger but not knowing what that is. In 2006 I established LifeSculpt, offering one-on-one coaching and workshop facilitation to help women live not by default, but by design.

My life experience includes piloting an airplane, teaching meditation, assisting lawyers and judges, tap dancing, life coaching, novel writing and pottery. I have read the self-help books, done the exercises, and navigated the personal turbulence of trial and error. I have sifted out the simple, essential gems that produce stunning results for myself and my clients, and I have set them out in my book, *Full Bloom: 7 Practical Steps to Get What You Want +1 to Grow On.*

I believe it is important to laugh, especially at ourselves.

My guiding principle: Don't take yourself too seriously!

My secret to living happily ever after: Appreciate.

Visit Nina online at www.NinaDurfee.com.

Anna Goldsworthy

Since I was six years old, I remember people stopping to celebrate my smile. So far, life has provided me many opportunities to embrace intense joy and to survive heartbreaking challenge. Through it all, my most cherished keepsake is my understanding that the exchange of a natural smile creates value, compassion, and power—the giver and receiver are equally blessed.

Retreating to coach with women is a similar phenomenon. Those who treat themselves to the very intimate and life-enhancing experience of our retreats, workshops, and private sessions form a unique and powerful connection creating mutual benefit for everyone involved. I am honored to listen, reflect, and hold space for joy, clarity, and purpose with clients who have in common a strong belief that personal growth is not a luxury but, like air, water, and a natural smile, is a necessity to survive and thrive in the world today!

I believe in the power of imagination and the freedom of possibility.

My guiding principle comes from none other than Dr. Seuss, who said: "Be who you are and say what you feel, because those who mind don't matter and those who matter don't mind."

Visit Anna online at www.PossibilityDetective.com.

Index of Questions

Made in the USA
San Bernardino, CA
16 October 2013